FEDERAL BUREAU OF PRISONS

Making Changes

I0455944

A Program of Hope, FCI Cumberland

Making Changes

SUPPORTING A SUCCESSFUL TRANSITION to the community is central to the mission of the Bureau of Prisons.

Read about some of the ways the Bureau protects public safety by helping inmates prepare for productive, crime-free lives after release.

FCI MEMPHIS INMATES
GIVE BACK INMATES SERVING LONG SENTENCES MENTOR YOUNGER INMATES

Some FCI Memphis inmates are working hard to help others learn from their mistakes. Mentors For Life, is the brain child of inmates Theodore Varner, Philander Butler, and Associate Wardens Dewayne Hendrix and Robert Stock. In 2013, realizing they had several decades to serve in prison, Mr. Varner and Mr. Butler wanted to help young inmates understand the importance of changing their behavior and their thinking patterns in order to change their destiny. Under the direction of Bobby Hager, Reentry Coordinator, Mr. Varner and Mr. Butler began hosting weekly meetings with approximately 20 inmates, to share their life stories and encourage the younger inmates to take a different path. Since that time, the program has grown in popularity and now is a 10 week program offered throughout the year. More than 100 inmates have successfully completed the program.

...encourage the younger inmates to take a different path.

SEEKING TRANSFORMATION BEHIND BARS
MAN PROGRAM HAS POSITIVE IMPACT ON MEN'S LIVES

It began with one inmate's vision to help his peers transform themselves by renewing their minds. Inmate Antonio Oesby, alongside Counselor Paul Marerro, developed the Mentality Adjustment Now (MAN) program at FCI Hazelton. The program, currently in its third class, focuses on developing a healthy and cohesive sense of self by encouraging inmates to share personal stories to increase their own awareness of emotions and thoughts. Participating men recognize and confront underlying issues, and learn how to respond in a positive manner. The group meets once a week for 12-weeks and focuses on forgiveness, encouragement, decision-making, anger, resentment, and dignity. The final session of the program focuses on the future and creating a positive path forward.

...focuses on developing a healthy and cohesive sense of self...

The change is real as noted by inmate Mark Thompson, a recent graduate, who describes the course as "ripping the blanket off of the past and facing it head on." Another recent graduate, inmate Dean Winslade, sums up his experience by saying "forgiveness is freedom" and he has learned to make his incarceration a more "redemptive time."

A PROGRAM OF HOPE
FCI CUMBERLAND HOSTS A UNIQUE SUMMER CAMP

In August, 2015, twelve children ages 9 - 14 spent five hours a day with their dads working on art projects, playing games, dancing, writing poetry and strengthening relationships. The fathers are inmates at the Federal Correctional Institution, Cumberland, Maryland, who were selected to participate in an annual arts-based father and child summer camp.

The five-day camp brings in local artists to help fathers and children create an "art story" of their lives. Each family paints a giant (8'x10') mural that depicts a perfect day together - what would they be doing if dad was not in prison. Sometimes the murals portray a positive memory of past activity together. Other families choose to create a mural that represents a dream of something they would like to do together. This year in addition to visual arts, the families worked with a poet to write poetry together.

While working on the art projects each family has time time to talk and catch up on each other's lives. They share hopes and dreams and often rebuild relationships strained and sometimes shattered by incarceration. During the past 14 years two children have met their fathers for the first time at camp.

The camp is sponsored by a DC based organization that helps incarcerated dads stay connected to their children. This summer in addition to Cumberland both FCI Big Spring and FCI Dublin hosted summer camps.

FPC MONTGOMERY HOLDS
REENTRY EVENT INMATES MEET WITH PROBATION OFFICERS AND ASSISTANT US ATTORNEYS

More than one hundred inmates participated in a highly successful reentry event at the Federal Prison Camp (FPC) in Montgomery, Alabama. Two U.S. Probation Officers, and two U.S. Attorneys from the District of Georgia facilitated the event, focused on the importance of inmates changing their lives while in prison.

...focused on the importance of inmates changing their lives while in prison.

After the presentation, the panel met with approximately 25 inmates who are releasing to the Middle District of Georgia. The panelists met with inmates, one-on-one, to discuss issues or concerns the inmates raised relating to release. Some of the inmates asked general questions regarding courses they could take while still in prison (or at an RRC) that would better enable them to obtain employment when released, and they also inquired about employers in Georgia that would hire ex-felons.

KEEPING THE WHEELS TURNING
MARION INMATES REFURBISH BIKES FOR THE COMMUNITY

Inmates at the United States Penitentiary (USP) satellite camp in Marion, Illinois, are helping to provide bicycles to children in the community. The institution partners with a local not-for-profit organization that provides safety classes and free bikes to children.

Inmates inspect used bikes provided by the local organization, checking the safety of parts such as the brakes, chain, tires and steering. The inmates then make any needed repairs; each bicycle is essentially rebuilt by the time it leaves USP Marion. "This program gives the inmates vocational training that can be used upon release," said Aubray Bailey, the Executive Assistant and Camp Administrator at USP Marion. "It also gives the inmates an avenue to give back to the community while they are incarcerated."

"It also gives the inmates an avenue to give back to the community while they are incarcerated."

Since 2010, inmates at the minimum security camp have refurbished over 3,000 bikes for local children.

WOMEN'S RELATIONSHIPS
GENDER-RESPONSIVE PROGRAM AT FPC BRYAN

Female inmates at the Federal Prison Camp, Bryan, Texas, have a unique opportunity to address the challenges of incarceration and to address some of the issues that led to their involvement in the criminal justice system. To date approximately 100 women have participated in the structured intervention program entitled "Women's Relationships." This program assists female inmates in understanding and maintaining healthy connections within and outside prison.

A recent graduate of the program, Dora Arreguy, noted that many of the women at Bryan have relationship issues or hurdles to overcome, and she believes the class helped each one in a different way: "It helped me realize that I need to do what is best for my relationship with myself before I can expect to move forward to better relationships with others."

Marne Boyle, Warden at Bryan and leader of the treatment group, emphasized the need for individual engagement with the inmates: "You can read about women all day, but you really get to know them as people and understand their struggles when you lead them in programs."

Women's Relationships is an important program for female inmates in the Bureau of Prisons, many of whom cite unhealthy relationships as their pathway to prison.

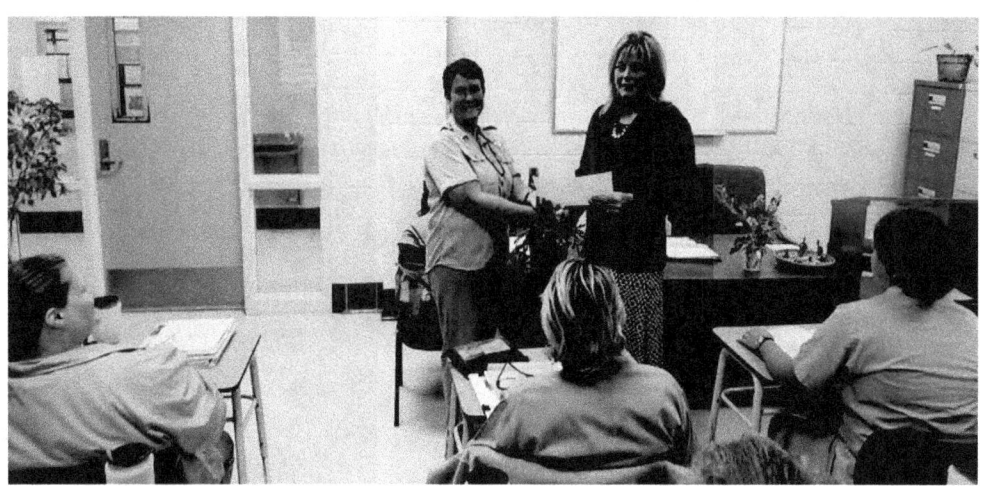

FTC OKLAHOMA CITY HAS ONE-OF-A-KIND MISSION

MORE THAN 85,000 INMATES A YEAR PASS THROUGH THE FEDERAL TRANSFER CENTER

In 2015, approximately 86,000 inmates passed through the Federal Transfer Center (FTC) in Oklahoma City, Oklahoma, on the way to their designated institutions across the country. Since its activation in 1995, more than 1.7 million inmates have been processed through the facility.

"We are the only institution in the Bureau with this unique, multifaceted mission," said Chad Garrett, the Executive Assistant at FTC Oklahoma City. "Operations are busy, with our receiving and discharge section processing inmates 24 hours a day, 5 days a week."

The FTC temporarily houses approximately 1,500 male and female inmates with an average stay of approximately 30 days. There are 175 low security inmates designated to the FTC to perform a range of duties throughout the facility.

FTC Oklahoma City is located at the Will Rogers World Airport and is an integral component of the U.S. Marshals' prisoner operations. The FTC works closely with the USMS' Justice Prisoner & Alien Transportation System (JPATS), which is responsible for coordinating the transfer of inmates throughout the country.

The Federal Bureau of Prisons currently has 122 institutions nationwide; however FTC Oklahoma City is the only one of its kind with its unique and vital mission.

MORE ACCESS TO REENTRY INFORMATION FOR INMATES AND OTHERS

INMATES TO BE PROVIDED WITH COMMUNITY-SPECIFIC RESOURCE INFORMATION

The Bureau of Prisons has provided inmates a new opportunity to access information critical to making release plans. Inmates can now access the Fair Shake Reentry Resource Center's information on a DVD being provided to each federal prison at no cost. The DVD contains community-specific resources on employment, housing, healthcare, transportation, food, clothing, and benefits.

Fair Shake resources are also accessible via the organization's internet website for friends and families to access https://www.fairshake.net.

The Bureau of Prisons does not endorse or support the information or services offered by any organization.

SECURE STAGES EVIDENCE-BASED TREATMENT FOR SUCCESSFUL MANAGEMENT OF MENTAL ILLNESS

Maximum security inmates with personality disorders and a history of self-injurious behavior or with a history of not functioning effectively in a prison setting have new programming opportunities in federal prisons. The Secure STAGES Program, modeled after the Stages Program that was developed at the Federal Correctional Complex (FCC) Terre Haute, has been expanded to the United States Penitentiary (USP) Florence where it has been well received. This residential treatment program targets inmates who have historically been difficult to manage in the prison environment, and provides them an opportunity to address their mental illness and learn skills needed to function effectively in prison and the community.

Secure STAGES has a locked side and an open side, thereby allowing inmates to participate in treatment while they are enhancing their ability to function in a more open setting. While in the program, which lasts for a minimum of 12 months, inmates learn to manage intense emotions, use rational thinking, and build positive relationships.

...provides them an opportunity to address their mental illness and learn skills needed to function effectively...

Aaron Stone, one of the 12 participants in the program at USP Florence, finds the program extremely beneficial: "[The] Secure STAGES Program has been everything to me; given me hope and optimism for the future." Brian Murray, another participant, also finds the program effective: "Secure STAGES is highly beneficial to one's needs to gain the proper tools to join society and to be productive while incarcerated."

INMATES COMMIT TO BE FIT WORKING TOWARD A HEALTHY LIFESTYLE

A group of inmates at the Federal Correctional Institution in Cumberland, Maryland are helping other inmates be healthier and more physically fit. The Recreation and Health Services staff at FCI Cumberland are working with inmate instructors to teach inmates about the risks associated with a sedentary lifestyle and show inmates how to be more active and productive. Inmates participate in the Weight Management class where they learn the principles of healthy weight loss, the importance of a healthy exercise routine, nutrition and dietary needs and how to improve their overall nutritional health. Mr. Phares is a shining example of what can be accomplished with hard work and a commitment to change. He was a participant in the Introduction to Weight Management program from January 2014 through Summer 2015; he lost 28 pounds, and makes healthy food selections during mainline and better choices from the commissary. Mr. Phares says he is the healthiest he has been since the beginning of his incarceration.

...show inmates how to be more active and productive.

RECIDIVISM DATA SHOWS
16% DECLINE NEW USSC DATA REFLECTS RECIDIVISM DOWN

On March 9, 2015, the United States Sentencing Commission (USSC), released a comprehensive report on recidivism among federal offenders. Their report focused on the number of inmates from 2005 that were rearrested within eight years for a new crime or for a violation of the conditions of their probation or release Recidivism is most commonly defined as rearrest for a new crime or revocation of supervision within three years after release from prison. While not published in the USSC report, at the request of the Bureau, the USSC reported this traditional recidivism measure: only 33.7% of the inmates released from the Bureau of Prisons in 2005 were rearrested or had their supervision revoked over a three year period. This figures reflects a 16% decline compared to historic Bureau of Prisons rates of recidivism and compares favorably to the rate of 67.8 percent average rate across the largest states.The staff in the Bureau of Prisons work with inmates from the first day of incarceration to prepare for a successful return to the community; these efforts are paying off. The complete USSC report can be viewed here: http://www.ussc.gov/news/press-releases-and-news-advisories/march-9-2016

PARTNERSHIP IN POLICY REACHES MILESTONE
100 POLICIES ISSUED IN UNDER THREE YEARS

The Bureau of Prison's labor and management Partnership reached another major milestone this week when the 100th policy was published in three years. These 100 new policies represent more than a quarter of all the agency's existing policies, and more than 30 additional policies are in development.

In late 2013, the Bureau's Executive Staff and the Council of Prison Locals agreed on the formation of nine Joint Policy Committees (JPCs) to reinvigorate the policy development process in the agency. These JPCs have worked tirelessly to produce more policies in three years than had been done in the prior decade. Congratulations to everyone involved in policy development, and especially to the members of the JPCs whose dedication to the principles of Partnership have put the Bureau's policy process firmly back on track.

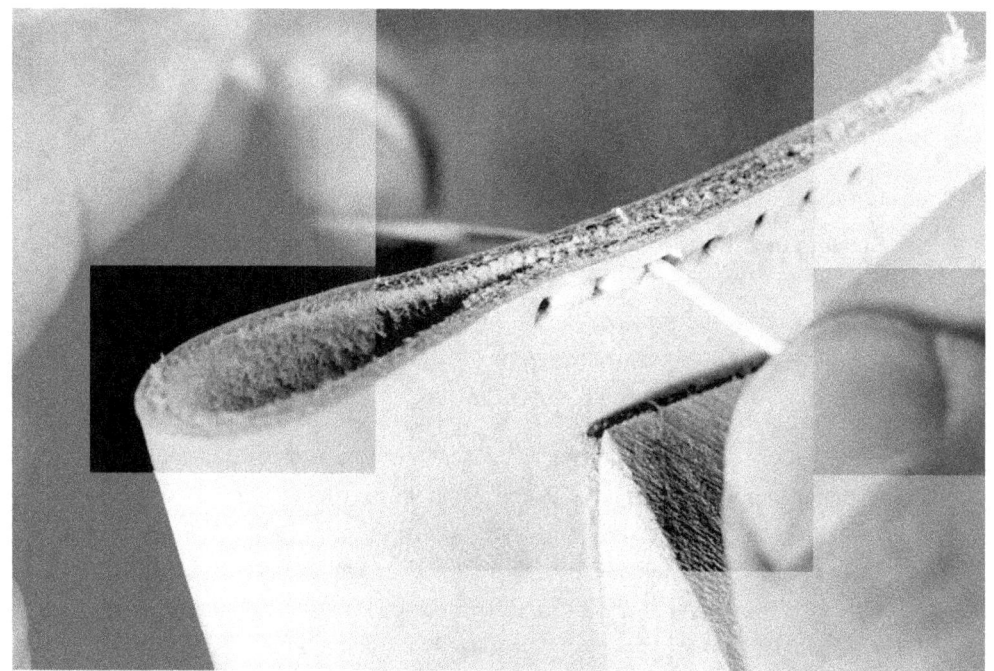

HIDDEN ART
LOCKED AWAY INMATES TAKE PRIDE IN THEIR CREATIVITY

USP Leavenworth inmates Terry Manning and John Glenn take pride in working with other inmates to develop their creative talents. Through a 12-week course, supervised by Recreation Supervisor Terence Avery, these two men teach other inmates how to make beautiful craft items. Many of the items are given to children at a local children's hospital in Kansas City, and other items are displayed at an annual community art show. USP Leavenworth inmates have had items in the show for more than 35 years. This year inmates displayed 69 paintings, 15 drawings, and 91 leather-craft items. The show, "Hidden Art Locked Away," was held on February 2, 2016 at a local community center in Leavenworth, Kansas.

...working with other inmates to develop their creative talents.

INSIGHT A NEW TOOL FOR CASE MANAGERS

Starting next month, some case managers will have a new tool to create individualized reentry plans for inmates. And, for the first time, treatment staff and work detail supervisors will have an automated way to provide input to the case managers who prepare the plans.

These tools, Insight, and the companion program Feedback, are fully integrated with the on-line information system used by the Bureau of Prisons to provide its operational and management information requirements (SENTRY) and have been developed collaboratively by management and labor. A Joint Policy Committee (JPC), with participants from the Information, Policy and Public Affairs (IPPA), Reentry Services, and Correctional Programs Divisions, along with Subject Matter Experts from various field sites have been involved in every step of the development process.

In addition to creating progress reviews and reports, staff will use Insight to prepare Residential Reentry Center Referrals and other types of release packets. Staff will route documents electronically, including submitting the packet to the appropriate Residential Reentry Management Office.

Insight is operational at the Low Security Correctional Institution, Allenwood, Pennsylvania. The system will be rolled out to the Allenwood complex next month and eventually throughout the agency.

MILKING EVERY OPPORTUNITY FOR SUCCESSFUL REENTRY
INMATES LEARN FARMING SKILLS AT FCI EL RENO

Dairy farming is not typically associated with prison life. But for many inmates at the FCI El Reno Satellite Camp, milking cows, bottle feeding newborn calves and tending to the herd are part of a daily routine that helps prepare them for viable job opportunities upon reentry into their communities.

Inmates working at the FCI El Reno dairy learn skills from Federal Prison Industries staff, all of whom have farming backgrounds. Dairy Farmer Foreman George Wylie enjoys teaching inmates the skills he learned working on family farms and for major farming companies. Inmate Christopher Prado hopes to turn this experience into a job working on one of the many dairy farms near his home; an opportunity he passed up as a child, while his grandfather owned a beef cattle operation. Another inmate, Stefan James, has obtained a Commercial Driver License during incarceration and currently delivers milk to 18 institutions in the South Central Region. He plans to continue working as a truck driver when he is released.

...helps prepare them for viable job opportunities upon reentry....

The dairy operation at El Reno includes 490 dairy cows and produces approximately 3,100 gallons of milk each day.

FPC ALDERSON'S ALL-FEMALE INMATE FIRE BRIGADE

INMATE FIRE BRIGADE PROTECTS FEDERAL PROPERTY AND ASSISTS THE LOCAL COMMUNITY

Last year, the Bureau's only female inmate fire brigade responded to a church fire in Alderson, West Virginia. With the assistance of the inmate firefighters, the three other responding fire crews were able to contain the fire to one room of the church, with only smoke and water damage to the remaining areas. Thanks to the quick actions of the skilled firefighting crew, 1 church was preserved.

The Alderson Federal Prison Camp (FPC) Federal Fire Department 25 provides firefighting services for the Camp, as well as being a backup for local volunteer fire departments in the community. The FPC trains an all-volunteer, all-female inmate fire brigade, and has been doing so for over 38 years. Each year, approximately 25 inmates are selected from the list of volunteers and assigned to the FPC Alderson Fire Department. They are screened for the program and receive the same training, instruction, and certifications required of volunteer fire fighters in the community. In addition to giving back to the community, inmates learn valuable skills that can assist them in making a successful transition back into the community.

In addition to giving back to the community, inmate learn valuable skills that can assist them in making a successful transition back into the community.

REDUCING, REUSING OR RECYCLING
FCI MARIANNA INMATES
HELP RECYCLE TONS OF MATERIAL

In 2015, FCI Marianna prevented nearly 8 million pounds of materials from being sent to the landfill by using its recycling program run by Federal Prison Industries (also known as UNICOR). Inmates at the Florida institution were able to successfully recycle nearly 94 percent of the materials received into the program that may have otherwise been sent to nearby landfills.

The UNICOR program recycles electronics, cardboard, aluminum and many other metals. Female inmates at the adjacent minimum security satellite camp sort through most incoming shipments first; however, some shipments are

sent directly to the male inmates at the FCI. During the separating process, inmates remove all recyclable materials, such as wiring, mother boards, plastic, gold, and copper. The materials are then sorted by type, and sent out to vendors who have purchased the recyclables from UNICOR. Materials which cannot be recycled are then sent to the landfill.

...successfully recycle nearly 94 percent of the materials received into the program that may have otherwise been sent to nearby landfills.

In this age of diminishing resources, tight budgets, and environmental concerns, staff and inmates in FCI Marianna's recycling program are working together to reduce the amount of material sent to landfills and to improve the world we live in.

INSIDE-OUT
PRISON EXCHANGE PROGRAM
FOCUSING ON REENTRY FROM THE INSIDE-OUT

In 2010, FCC Hazelton became the first BOP institution to host the Inside-Out Prison Exchange Program that allows prisoners and college students to benefit from studying crime, justice and related social issues together as peers. Over the past 5 1/2 years, 115 inmates (male and female) have participated, along with over 150 college students from West Virginia University and Fairmont State University. The inmates and college students meet once per week, for an entire semester, reading text books and writing papers. In addition, the class develops a project, generally geared toward re-entry initiatives.

...an "opportunity to be part of the solution of our failures"...

The Inside-Out program enables college students to gain perspective on the criminal justice system, and inmates an opportunity to place their life experiences in a larger framework. Inmate participant Dwight Harrison from FCC Hazleton, views Inside-Out as an "opportunity to be part of the solution of our failures" and thinks of it as an "extension of usefulness in a world full of learned helplessness."

In 2013, Inside-Out was implemented at FCI Morgantown, and now, nearing the end of its 4th class, 31 WVU students and 31 inmates have participated.

HOPE FOR INTEGRATION
REINTEGRATION HOUSING UNIT (RHU)

FCC Oakdale's Reintegration Housing Unit (RHU) helps protective custody inmates learn to live in open prison populations. Specifically, inmates are taught about anxiety management, relationship building and self-confidence.

RHU targets inmates who have difficulty functioning in the prison environment and have fears of being around other inmates. Participants complete three phases of programming which lasts for a minimum of 6 months in a dedicated unit, apart from the rest of the inmate population.

"It taught me about my hidden strengths and to equip me to make a positive reintegration back to society."

The program currently is being expanded to USP Atwater and USP Coleman I.

Inmate Thomas McDonald, one of the graduates and currently a program mentor in the RHU, explained that the unit provides a "safe environment to learn how to think rationally, and overcome adversity. It taught me about my hidden strengths and to equip me to make a positive reintegration back to society."

VETERANS LIVE AND LEARN TOGETHER

FCI MORGANTOWN PAVES PATH FOR SUCCESSFUL REENTRY

Inmate-veterans at the Federal Correctional Institution, Morgantown, WV, have their own living space, where they participate in programming conducted by volunteers from local support agencies. They receive assistance in obtaining medical and military records, health benefits, employment needs, and VA pension rules. Special classes are conducted in Anger Management, PTSD, Life Experiences, Readjustment, Relationships and Life Skills.

Currently, there are inmate-veterans representing the Army, Navy, Air Force and Marines, residing in the Veterans' Wing. The program is facilitated by John Gribble and Brian Plavi, both Correctional Counselors and military veterans themselves.

Wing

Inmate-veterans who reside in the Veterans' Wing have the opportunity to become certified service dog trainers. Through the Veterans-to-Veterans Service Dog Program , in collaboration with West Virginia University's (WVU) Division of Animal and Nutritional Sciences Department and Hearts of Gold Service Dog Certification Program, inmate-veteran dog trainers can achieve various levels of certification. Once training is complete, the dogs are placed with veterans in the community who have mobility impairments and/or Post Traumatic Stress Disorder (PTSD).

FCI Morgantown provides them with a "sense of comradeship with others who are former military,"

Inmate-veterans George Cannady and Tony Newton, are dog trainers, and agree that the Veterans Program at FCI Morgantown provides them with a "sense of comradeship with others who are former military," and the opportunity to "obtain up-to-date information on benefits and services offered by the Veterans' Administration." Since the program's inception in 2011, more than 350 veteran-inmates have benefited from this unique program.

BIG SPRING STAFF
SAVE INMATE'S LIFE
TRAINING HELPS FIRST RESPONDERS BE PREPARED

On February 27, 2016, staff at the Federal Correctional Institution in Big Spring, Texas saved the life on an inmate who had suffered a heart attack. Recreation Specialists Kerry Edwards Jr., Ronald Barber, Concepcion Serrato and Senior Officer Specialist John Meyer responded to a call for a medical emergency, and upon arriving at the scene they found an inmate lying on the floor, unresponsive. They immediately began to administer CPR and called for medical support. The nurse on duty, Alison Murphree, responded and used an automated external defibrillator (AED) and provided oxygen to the inmate who had known to suffer from cardiac issues. Emergency Medical Technicians from the community arrived within 12 minutes and were able to transfer the inmate to a local hospital in stable condition.

The staff at Big Spring worked as a team during the medical emergency and used the CPR and other training they are provided at the institution to save a life.

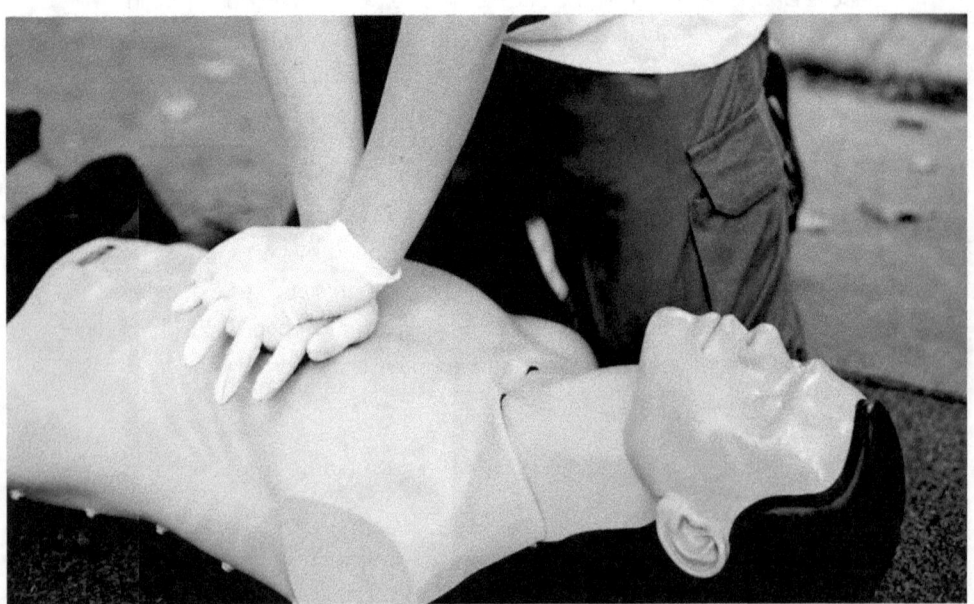

INMATES RECEIVE VT CERTIFICATION
PROGRAM PROVIDES INMATES WITH REENTRY OPPORTUNITIES

Last year, 53 out of 57 inmates enrolled in the building trades program at the Federal Correctional Institution, Phoenix, Arizona, passed the Vocational Training (VT) exam provided by the National Occupational Competency Testing Institute (NOCTI); this is a higher passing rate than the national average!

Through 240 hours of coursework, inmates learn a variety of skills that can lead to high paying jobs in the community, including careers in carpentry, electrical, and plumbing. Students who pass the NOCTI test are placed in a national registry database with the Home Builders Association that enables future employers to verify individual's credentials when he or she is applying for employment. The registry also allows individuals to post a resume online that will reach a national audience of future employers (inmates have access to this service after release to the community).

...inmates learn a variety of skills that can lead to high paying jobs in the community...

Inmate Jardon Laforcarde, noted that the training improves job prospects because of "the amount of hands on experience we receive and receiving an industry recognized certificate." VT Instructor Joe Kavenaugh is certified to proctor exams through the National Home Builders Association and National Occupational Career Training Institute. His certification, advanced skills, and expertise has a positive impact on this reentry VT program.

LESSONS FOR SUCCESS
FORMER EDGEFIELD INMATE
RETURNS TO TALK ABOUT RDAP

Former inmate Walter Pavlo completed the Residential Drug Abuse Program (RDAP) in 2003 and since that time has devoted his life to assisting others on both sides of the fence.

Mr. Pavlo recently returned to the Satellite Prison Camp at Edgefield and spoke to current RDAP inmates. "My participation in RDAP represented the first time in my entire life that I really reflected on my life, both the good and the bad." One of his most important messages to the current inmates was to start preparing for release as soon as you arrive, through whatever means are available. "The lessons I learned during RDAP helped when I needed patience to continue to recover from the mistakes that I made and prepare for the successes that were ahead and the people I met during RDAP, both inmates and staff, made me a better person than the one who entered prison."

"...the first time in my entire life that I really reflected on my life, both the good and the bad."

The lessons learned by Mr. Pavlo helped him become a successful entrepreneur. He has been invited to speak to the FBI, US Attorney's Office, major corporations and at over 100 colleges and universities, and he has had guest appearances on many television shows.

COOKING UP CHANGE
FCI FORT DIX PARTNERSHIP
SUPPORTS REENTRY EFFORTS

Camp inmates at the Federal Correctional Institution, Fort Dix, New Jersey participate in a unique culinary arts program that not only prepares them for potential careers, but also provides valuable life skills. This training program has an 81 percent job placement rate in the food service industry.

"You just don't learn how to cook, you learn how to approach life."

The program begins with two weeks of training focusing on life skills, job preparation, and personal finance. The inmates then participate in the 14-week culinary arts vocational training program. Upon completion, the inmates also participate in an internship in the community. The class valedictorian for this program has been a BOP inmate in each of the three graduating classes since Fort Dix began participating. Inmate Zarwea Sehneah said the program, "is a great place to help start over again. You just don't learn how to cook, you learn how to approach life." Inmate Ali Burke states, "It is an outstanding program that I plan to use to hopefully start a new career in culinary arts."

DRIVING REENTRY HOME
FORMER PETERSBURG INMATE
ENJOYS THE SUCCESS OF HIS EFFORTS

Johnny Sauls was an inmate at the Federal Prison Camp in Petersburg, Virginia in 2011 when he obtained his Commercial Driver's License (CDL). In September 2015, he returned to the Federal Correctional Complex (FCC) Petersburg to share his reentry success story at the CDL Recognition Ceremony, inspiring inmates currently in the program.

In 2010, FCC Petersburg began piloting the CDL Program. After obtaining his CDL (the first inmate to do so), Mr. Sauls became the lead instructor for the institution's CDL program, while still incarcerated at the camp. He provided general knowledge and classroom instruction on pre-trip inspections, air brakes, and behind-the-wheel driving. He assisted more than 50 inmates in studying and preparing to obtain their Class A and B licenses, before

"The CDL is one of the best programs that the BOP had to offer. It gave me a sense of hope, accomplishment..."

he was transferred to a Residential Reentry Center (RRC) in North Carolina. Within two weeks of his arrival at the RRC, Mr. Sauls obtained a job with a trucking company. He is currently working full time, receiving health benefits for himself and his family, and has obtained his Hazmat Endorsement. When speaking of his time in the Bureau of Prisons, Mr. Sauls said, "The CDL is one of the best programs that the BOP had to offer. It gave me a sense of hope, accomplishment and ultimately a career in the trucking industry."

Since the inception of the program at FCC Petersburg, more than 100 inmates have obtained their Commercial Driver's License and with it, the potential for their own successful reentry.

FCI MORGANTOWN
OSHA TRAINING
COURSE PROVIDES INMATES COMPLETION CARD

On March 24, 2016, twenty-five (25) inmates at FCI Morgantown completed the institution's inaugural offering of OSHA-10. The Occupational Safety and Health Administration (OSHA) Outreach Training Program provides training to individuals in the recognition, avoidance, abatement, and prevention of safety and health hazards in the workplace. Among the courses offered in this program is "OSHA 10," which helps to ensure that entry-level workers are more knowledgeable about workplace hazards and their rights. OSHA issues to inmates who complete the course a course completion card, which is evidence to potential employers of course completion.

The OSHA Training Program is made available in partnership with the West Virginia University (WVU) Safety & Health Extension Department and OSHA. Stephen Fazenbaker, Safety Compliance Specialist and Authorized OSHA-10 Instructor, hopes to offer this course on a monthly basis.

...it's nice to have the course completion card as tangible proof of my completion of the course, as I re-enter the workforce."

Roger Alan Cornelison, an inmate who has completed numerous programs and courses during his time in prison and who was among the twenty-five (25) inmates recently completing the course, states: "The OSHA-10 course is one of the most informative, beneficial courses being offered, and it's nice to have the course completion card as tangible proof of my completion of the course, as I re-enter the workforce."

THE ART OF
THE SECOND CHANCE

Theomas Rhode, Owner and Chief Executive Officer of Ponchaveli Studios, released from the Federal Correctional Institution, Seagoville, Texas, just 6 years ago. While in prison, Rhodes completed his release portfolio (a long standing education department initiative) that began his successful transition to the community.

Shortly after releasing from prison, Mr. Rhodes interviewed for a maintenance worker position. Despite being told the company had a policy against hiring people with criminal backgrounds, Mr. Rhodes left a copy of his release portfolio and thanked the interviewer

"And this (release portfolio) outweighs this (criminal history rap sheet) any day."

for his time. A few days later, he received a second interview with the Human Resources Director. During the interview the HR Director pointed to Mr. Rhodes' criminal history record and said, "you have this, but you also have this (pointing at his release portfolio). And this (release portfolio) outweighs this (criminal history rap sheet) any day." She offered him the job, and over time Mr. Rhodes was promoted from maintenance worker to leasing agent.

Over the past six years, Mr. Rhodes has reestablished his relationship with his children, and pursued a successful career in art. He credits his artistic talent, the programs he took advantage of while he was incarcerated, and his release portfolio as essential elements leading to his success.

WRITING TRANSFORMS LIVES

4 P.M. COUNT SHOWCASES INMATE CREATIVE WRITING

Inmates at the Federal Prison Camp, Yankton, SD are coming to terms with the decisions that landed them in prison and are growing as individuals thanks to a unique writing program.

Dr. James Reese, Associate Professor of English at Mount Marty College in Yankton, and Kyle Roberson, Supervisor of Education have been collaborating on the program for the past nine years. "Writing transforms lives," says Dr. Reese. Inmate Marquise Bowie says that "this program has helped in [my] healing process," and he is thankful for the "opportunity to share part of [my] personal story in hopes that others can learn from [my] mistakes."

...coming to terms with the decisions that landed them in prison and are growing as individuals....

The Writer-In-Residence program, that lasts for 9-months and currently has 16 inmates participating, teaches inmates to communicate through writing, using the theory of "transformative justice." The program culminates in the annual publication of 4 P.M. Count, a showcase for the men's talents. The 2015 edition features 240 pages of creative work.

Writer-in-Residence is part of the Artist-in-Residence (AIR) program that provides inmates with exposure to professional artists. AIR is funded by the National Endowment for the Arts, and is currently running at six BOP institutions.

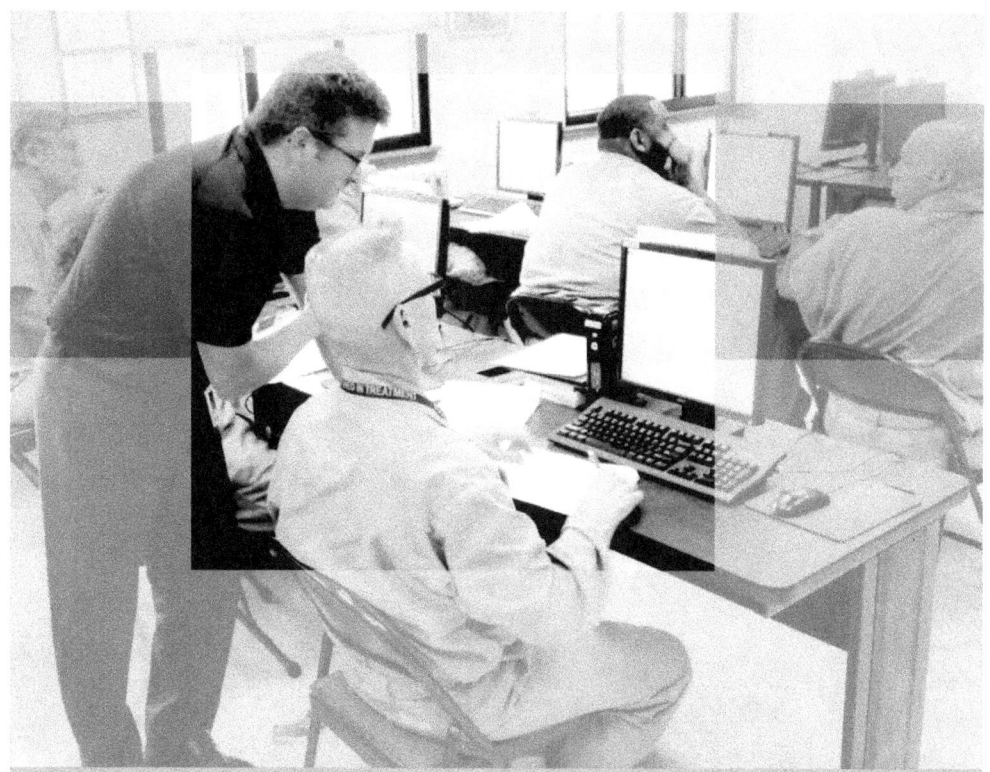

Writing Transforms Lives, Federal Prison Camp, Yankton, SD

www.ingramcontent.com/pod-product-compliance
Lightning Source LLC
Chambersburg PA
CBHW072026290526
45787CB00015B/2258